A Very

MODERN

Dictionary

A Very
MODERN
Dictionary

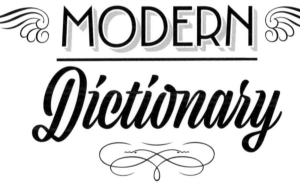

Over 400 words, phrases, acronyms & slang
to keep your culture game _on fleek_

Tobias Anthony

**Smith
Street
Books**

⇨ INTRODUCTION ⇦

Welcome, friends, to this very *modern* dictionary; a friendly guidebook to help you navigate the confusing and downright bewildering beast that is the ever-evolving English language.

We've trawled the darkest corners of the web, looking to bastions of modernity such as Reddit, *BuzzFeed* and the text messages of teenagers, which represent such a roiling mass of hyperbole and neologism it would make Shakespeare hang his head in defeat.

The very idea of a dictionary is to convey and to accurately represent language in its various stages of evolution, for language is in a constant state of flux, always moving and shifting and blending. The most common trend we noticed when compiling this book is an obsession with portmanteaus – hybrids that cobble together two words to make one new one. The evolution of language can often defy logic: the modern use of the word 'literally' is a perfect case in point, where it has now come to replace 'figuratively' despite the original meaning being its polar opposite. These quirks are what what makes language great. It is why culture is so fascinating.

We've also included a handy reference list of the most common acronyms, initialisms and abbreviations and their meanings, so you can tell your PIRs from your DTFs.

So please, turn the page and come on in, let us shine a light on over 400 modern words and phrases, to help you navigate the culture of our time.

a crapella

adjective

Singing out loud where no background music can be heard by the listener; someone singing aloud while listening to their headphones: *That girl in the library was making a total racket singing a crapella. She had no idea ...*

-ability

suffix

Indicates the degree to which something is suitable or capable. Currently being tacked on to just about any old word in a manner of reckless neology. See also **marketability**, **viewability** and **relatability**.

ad blocker

noun

Software designed to prevent advertisements from appearing on a web page. Ad blockers are a welcome resource to help fend off the knowledge that, through targeted advertising, Google can see deep into your personal data, maybe even your soul – ignorance is bliss!

adorkable

adjective

Portmanteau of *adorable* and *dork*. Someone socially inept, clumsy or with commonly perceived 'dorky' interests like video games or comic books, but who is also aesthetically adorable (at least, in the eye of the beholder): *Zooey Deschanel is soooo adorkable in* New Girl.

AF
phrase
Initialism of *as f@%k*; meaning 'intensely so': *Damn, that exam was hard AF.*

ain't nobody got time for that
phrase
Made popular by a viral video of the same name, in which a woman being interviewed about witnessing a house fire sums up the inconvenience of the ordeal, as well as the fact that she suffers from bronchitis, by stating simply, 'Ain't nobody got time for that.' The phrase was then co-opted by millions around the world as a catchall for dealing with the obstacles in their lives. If you're frustrated by the inconvenience of a task: *ain't nobody got time for that!*

amirite?
phrase
Contraction of *am I right?* Usually employed when affirming something, it's essentially asking, 'Agreed?', but when added to a sentence it serves to confirm the speaker's own opinion: *Bey still got the best booty, amirite?* Meaning, 'Beyonce Knowles has the best bottom and I'm right to say so, because it is true.'

ancient grains
noun
A variety of food sources including quinoa, chia, amaranth, millet and wild rice, as well as some forms

of wheat including spelt and farro. These grains have existed for a very long time (hence 'ancient') but have been rediscovered more recently by contemporary health and culinary experts. Essentially a marketing term used to imbue these grains and pseudocereals with an air of romanticism and mysticism to make them appear more nutritious and fancy.

and scene
phrase
A reference to a statement a dramatic actor might say at the conclusion of a performance, typically at the end of a monologue. In day-to-day usage, it's a sign-off indicating the momentous nature (ironically or otherwise) of what you've said or done.

... and then I found fifty dollars
phrase
Can be added to the end of any pointless, boring story to indicate your awareness of how pointless and boring your story turned out to be. If you're feeling bitchy, you can tack it onto the end of someone else's story, subsequently letting them know how you felt about having to listen to it.

Angry Birds
noun
A video game and mobile app that involves shooting irate birds from a sling shot at smug green pigs. One of the most downloaded games of all time, with at least 15 spin-off games, animated TV series and feature film adaptations, and countless book, toy, beverage and theme park derivations ... really, you needed to look this up?

apology tour
phrase

The apologies made (most typically) by celebrities
on various social media and news media platforms
following public outcry over a controversial comment or
action, necessitated by the rights of every social media
user to express their extreme and impassioned outrage,
and their subsequent need for immediate pacification:
*Did you guys get a load of Alec Baldwin's phony apology tour
after he called his daughter a 'rude, thoughtless pig'?*

archery party
noun

The latest trend in themed
parties, this is exactly what
it sounds like: a party where
people shoot arrows at targets
for fun. Potentially originating
from the now-recognised
cultural insensitivity represented
by the once-popular cowboys
and Indians party theme
and the subsequent need to
do *something* with all of those
bow and arrow-related party
decorations.

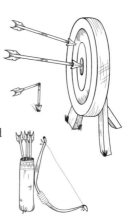

as
adverb

Emphasises the degree to which something is. When
applied to the end of an adjective it heightens the
preceding word: *easy as*, meaning 'really easy'; *hard as*,
meaning 'very hard'; and *simple as* meaning 'simples
pimples', or 'ain't no thang but a chicken wing'.

at the end of the day

phrase

The true point of contention or the point being made. Employed when highlighting your meaning in a conversation, usually your conclusion to a subject: *We could sit around and talk politics for hours, but, at the end of the day, I'll never regret voting for Trump.*

attention whore

noun

Someone who will do anything for attention or any person, regardless of gender, who seeks out attention – both good and bad – willingly. For example: any member of the Kardashian family.

awesomesauce

adjective

Something that is even more awesome than awesome: *I love bacon. Bacon is awesomesauce.*

awkward turtle

noun

A hand gesture deployed in awkward situations to communicate to the instigator that they're being inept. The gesture is made by placing the hands on top of one another and rotating the thumbs forward, thus animating the mascot of the awkward moment. Day-to-day usage: when a work colleague tells you a joke that's totes inappropes, just stay silent, perform the awkward turtle, then walk away.

bae
noun
Acronym for *before anyone else*, and shortened term for babe or baby; usually used to describe a significant other or best friend: *Props to my #bae for whipping up a bomb chicken and veg paleo soup.*

bafflegab
noun
Portmanteau of *baffling* and *gab*; any incomprehensible or pretentious verbiage, but most especially bureaucratic speech.

baller
noun / adjective
A rockstar; someone with confidence and swag. Originating from sports terms like footballer or basketballer, where those words are associated with icons who exude macho coolness. Describes something extremely impressive: *That time you planked on top of the Empire State Building was a total baller move.*

Bank of Mum and Dad
phrase
Describes a grown-up child who is financially supported by their parents: *Taking a loan from the Bank*

of Mum and Dad. Generally used as a derisive statement aimed at Millennials supported in their early adult years by their Generation X parents. Unsurprisingly, it is the same Gen X parents who are attributed with coining the phrase.

basic
adjective
Devoid of any characteristics that make a person (often female) in any way interesting; specifically pertaining to tastes and interests deemed beige, bland and boring: *She likes scented candles and sauvignon blanc and she even owns a picture frame with the word 'family' across the top – what a basic bitch.*

bee-tee-dubs
phrase
The latest way to stylise *BTW*, an initialism of *by the way*. Not only is it longer to type, making it less functional to use, it's also completely stupid, which is why all the cool cats be doing it: *Bee-tee-dubs you guys, I am going to seriously bring the lulz to this party tonight.*

Belieber
noun
A title that identifies anybody who understands fundamentally that Justin Bieber is the one true messiah.

believe that

phrase

Meaning, 'it's true', only with one-hundred times the power; employed at the end of a statement to let people know that there is no denying what you've just said: *If King Kong were around today, I'm sure I could kick his ass. Believe that.*

BF

noun

Short for *boyfriend*: *Me and the BF are totes excited to come see you after our CrossFit sesh tomorrow!* See also **GF**.

BFF

noun

Inititialism of *best friend forever*; that special someone in your life who you would do almost anything for. While your BFF can also be your BF or GF, this is rarely the context in which this is employed as it generally only refers to non-sexual relationships between people, aka, friends.

bi-line

phrase

The degree to which someone is bisexual. A metaphorical line where your sexuality starts to be less clearly defined. Everyone has a bi-line, but not everybody has crossed it. Discovering your bi-line can be greatly assisted by the consumption of tequila.

binge watching

verb

The act of consuming large amounts of visual media and/or content in a single (or short) period of time: *I binge watched all of* Game of Thrones *over the weekend.*

bleeding edge

noun

The leading edge of the leading edge; something so devastatingly new and advanced that saying 'cutting edge' just won't suffice.

#blessed

hashtag

Part of a social media post that acknowledges awareness of how lucky you are: *Mumma loves her nighttime cuddles in her Gucci sheets with her best and cutest bub #blessed.* Can also be used in verbal communication in its complete spoken form *hashtag blessed.*

boo

noun

Not what you yell when jumping out from behind a door, now a pet name for your significant other. Your boo is your girlfriend or boyfriend, your lover and bestie all in one. A little like bae, only not. It's *boo.*

BRB

phrase

Initialism of *be right back*, commonly employed in digital conversations between people where one person may have to be away from their screen or mobile device for a moment and conveys also their intention to return: *I gotta go potty … brb.*

Brexit

noun

Portmanteau of the words *British* and *exit;* the departure of the United Kingdom from the European Union, which occurred following a referendum in 2016.

bro code

noun

The understanding between bros on agreed upon actions and reactions to a variety of subjects and situations. For instance, the bro code stipulates that should a bro meet a particularly fine female at a party, you leave him alone regardless of the situation. If this bro drove you to the party and you need to leave, then you need to find your own way home without him.

broad

noun

Portmanteau of *bro code* and *road*; the subtle agreement or understanding between bro drivers that is sometimes displayed via actions such as affectionate nodding, waving to acknowledge 'thank you' or to simply say, 'hello', and allowing fellow bro drivers to swap lanes with ease: *When Jerry drove past Mike, though they had never met before, they waved to one another in accordance with the rules of the broad.* See also **bro code**.

bromance

noun

Portmanteau of *bro* and *romance*; a deep, platonic, non-sexual relationship between two (usually heterosexual) males. Think any movie starring Paul Rudd, Vince Vaughan and/or Jonah Hill.

burn

noun

An accurate and/or witty criticism so incisive it generally leaves you with no ability to rebut. Sometimes, for added emphasis, referred to as an *ice burn,* to indicate the cold-heartedness of the insult.

BuzzFeed
noun

A website originally known for its proficient use of hyperbole, clickbait headlines and funny cat memes, it now appears to be the major news source for anyone with a smartphone, ranging from the 'Top 5 breakfast bowls you need to eat right now' to '63 things you didn't know about airstrikes in Syria'. It's probable that today, in passing conversation, you will hear a discussion relating to a *BuzzFeed* article. *Buzzfeed* is known for the 'listicles' (that is a list article) the site provides, whether lists of celebrities who have done *x*, or of fashion trends that are *y*. A good *Buzzfeed* article captures the attention of anyone who has ever been bored at work and that's pretty much everybody. So get familiar. See also **clickbait**, **listicles**.

Bye, Felicia.
phrase

Used to express total disinterest at the departure of someone detestable and/or insignificant, originating from the 1995 Ice Cube movie *Friday*: *She completely blanked me when I tried to neg her so I was all like, 'bye, Felicia'*. See also **Damn, Gina**.

can't even...

phrase

Signifies incomprehension or being indisposed, and sometimes a combination of the two. Meaning that you either cannot wrap your mind around something because it is stupid or too cute, or that you cannot deal with something, either because it would pain you to or because you're not in the right frame of mind. Can be employed in the positive where humour is concerned: *I'm laughing so hard I literally can't even.* Can be employed negatively to describe being at a loss for words: *What was that? I can't even...*

cancel

verb

To reject something. You can cancel a person, place or thing: *You don't like Jenny because she's annoying? Just go ahead and cancel that girl from your life.* You don't feel like doing your homework? *Don't worry, your homework is cancelled, forget it.*

catfish

noun

A person who pretends to be somebody else online, either by hacking into someone's social media accounts or by creating false accounts under a fake identity.

celebrity chef

noun

A cultural phenomenon that really took off in the 2000s following the rise in popularity of cooking shows, competitive cooking-related reality television and programs that involve chefs swearing at hapless business owners, this title refers to cooks who have been elevated to rock star status, so that we may worship them as gods among men.

Chastain

noun

To be overrated yet highly visible, *a la* actress Jessica Chastain: *That Gwyneth Paltrow is such a Chastain.*

#checkyourprivilege

hashtag

An attachment to a social media post intended to draw attention to the privileges of people from Western capitalist societies, most especially those who make up the middle-class majority. This group are commonly thought to lack an appreciation of the lifestyle into which they have been born, in which they enjoy enormous privilege where race, education and socio-economic status are concerned, compared to the vast majority of the global population. Unfortunately now commonly misappropriated by that same group and used as a way to diffuse what is clearly an insufferable humblebrag: *Embracing that #boholife for the rest of the holidays with #messyhair and #lazymornings. Whatever you do, do it with your whole #spirit. #wanderlust #checkyourprivilege.* See also **#blessed**, **humblebrag.**

chillax
verb
Portmanteau of *chill* and *relax*; to calm down or spend some quiet time doing very little: *'What do you feel like doing today?' 'Not much. Just chillaxing.'* or *'Hey dude, you really need to chillax.'*

chopped and screwed
phrase
To change drastically; originally used to refer to the remixing of hip-hop music: *That dope-ass track got chopped and screwed.* Now commonly used in a broader context with regard to inebriation – as in the changing or altering of one's state via the consumption of alcohol and/or illicit drugs: *I went out on the weekend and got completely chopped and screwed.*

#chosen
hashtag
An attachment to a social media post, often with a traditional religious context but also commonly used to describe a state of smug enlightenment and a sense of feeling hand-picked by a god-like being for a specified task, or being selected by fate to experience good fortune: *Just got the last paleo superfood bar at my fav brunch spot! #chosen.* See also **#blessed**.

chronotype

noun

Behavioural classification based on underlying circadian rhythms; a person's propensity to sleep at a particular time during a twenty-four hour period. In other words, a fancy, sciency way of saying whether or not you are a morning person.

cis / cisgender

adjective

Those who identify with the gender that aligns with their birth sex; not transgender. *Cis* is Latin for 'on this side of' and *trans* for 'across, beyond, or on the other side of'.

clickbait

noun

A sensational online headline (or combination of headline and image) that is very carefully constructed to rouse your curiosity and manipulate you into clicking on a link. Specifically deployed to increase page views and hence generate online advertising revenue. Can be used in broader contexts to describe any attention-seeking or sensationalist activity or behaviour: *Did you see Rihanna's 'nude' dress at the MET Gala? So clickbait.*

clusterf@#k

phrase

An event of a disastrous nature, something that was extremely difficult or went badly; usually with the implication of a convergence of smaller disasters that lead to a catastrophic bigger picture: *Yesterday, absolutely everything that could go wrong, did go wrong; it was a complete and total clusterf@#k.*

Columbusing

verb

When white people claim to have 'discovered' something that has been known for some time by non-white people. Originating from comedy website *College Humor*, it refers to explorer Christopher Columbus's 'discovery' of the Americas, despite the fact that the significant native populations were probably aware of their own existence prior to this. In current usage, it refers to cultural practices, places and things that are 'discovered' by white people and subsequently co-opted by that community.

content

noun

Creative material such as writing, photography, animation, video, etc. required to feed the insatiable appetites of the internet. Those who produce this online content even call themselves *content creators*. As opposed to writers, photographers, animators, film makers, etc.

correct

phrase

Right beyond a shadow of a doubt; perfect. Commonly employed with regard to how you presents yourself and how you look. If you *come correct*, then you are looking sharp or on point. See also **on point**.

co-working space

noun

Space in which individuals or groups of people from various companies work together in an office-like environment. Evolved to suit the needs of a casualised workforce and the rise of start-ups and entrepreneurship. Most commonly found in converted warehouse spaces with identifying interior design features such as exposed brick walls, ping pong table, craft beer fridge and giant inspiring mural by a local street artist. See also **start-up**.

cray / craycray
phrase
Crazy, really crazy: *Todd's so craycray, he wants me to work over the weekend. That shit's cray!*

Cumberbitches
noun
Female fans of British actor Benedict Cumberbatch.

cyber bullying
verb
To harass, hurt or offend someone online, generally via social media platforms or email; usually used in relation to the harassment of children and teenagers (most commonly by other children and teenagers). Adults can be cyber bullied, too, we just don't like to call it that because we like to pretend that adults are more sophisticated than children.

dad bod
noun
A complimentary description used by those attracted to a man's body that is mostly lacking in muscle definition and may have a little bit of a paunch: *'Terry looks so great since he stopped going to the gym, he's got a total dad bod now.'*

dafuq
phrase
Abbreviation of *what the f@#k?*; mostly the result of internet memes, where the original phrase has been shortened, joined and spelled uniquely: *'You're a wizard, Harry.' 'Dafuq?'*

Damn, Gina.
phrase
Acknowledgement and/or approval of somebody doing or saying something impressive that you like: *'Did you see Callum threw a drink into cheating boyfriend's face?' 'Damn, Gina!'* See also **Bye, Felicia**.

dank
adjective
Of high quality, especially in reference to marijuana and memes: *Kind sir, I would like to know from where may I procure that dank herb?*

dark web

noun

Part of the internet that is accessible only by the use of special software that allows users to remain both anonymous and untraceable. You've probably heard of the dark web in some spy thriller, maybe you even  thought it was a Hollywood term made up to sound cool in the movies, but the dark web is actually a real thing.

dat boi

noun

A frog on a unicycle. *Trigger warning: If you cannot decipher the last sentence then do not attempt to do so, the discovery of what we're really talking about here may cause you to want to end your own life.

dead

adjective

1. When a celebrity is 'burnt' or 'slain' by another celebrity (via a tweet or social media attack) that celebrity dies socially and is thusly *dead*; 2. When someone makes you laugh so hard it practically kills you, you might want to tell them to stop joking around by saying *Stop, I'm dead!*; 3. When something such as a trend or cultural zeitgeist is officially 'over' it is *dead*.

deffo

Abbreviation of 'definitely': *'Are you going to check out the latest Tarantino movie?' 'Deffo.'*

derp
phrase
Used to highlight someone's mistake, whether an action or, more commonly, idiotic statement. *'Global Warming ain't real. I mean, yeah, sure, it's hotter this time of year than ever before, but it ain't real.' 'Derp.'*

DL
phrase
Initialism of *down low*; something that needs to be kept quiet and/or secret: *I hear Rebecca is pregnant, but you gotta keep that on the DL.* See also **low key**.

doe
adverb
Though. We're not sure how this works, it just does. It's just another thing that exists today, so make your peace and move on. Examples: We are providing no examples. This makes no sense. Don't use this word.

dope
adjective
Extremely cool and relevant. Ironically, the word itself is beginning to lose a bit of its dopeness, however, so maybe it's time to drop this one.

double rainbow
phrase
Intense joy, often coupled with extreme shifts in emotion – a balance of intense joy and melancholy or sadness. This phrase was born out of the reaction made by a hiker who, while stoned and looking to the sky, experienced a range of emotions while taking in the beauty of a double rainbow. Just look it up on YouTube.

douche / douchebag

noun

Obnoxious idiot; could be a colleague you can't stand or that person who won't stop trolling you online.

Dr Google

phrase

Using the internet (Google, specifically) to self-diagnose health issues. Generally considered an extremely bad idea: *'I'm pretty sure I have cancer. I read that elbow pain is a sign of cancer, for sure.' 'Really? Did Dr Google tell you that?'*

drag

verb

To rake someone over the coals; to put someone on blast. *Someone cuts in front of you in a line, you need to drag that mother to the ground.* See also **on blast**.

drank

adjective

The effect following the consumption of a cough syrup containing codeine and promethazine; a state not unlike being drunk, sought after by imbeciles.

dreams

interjection

An affirmative statement, expressing approval and delight; similar to 'good idea' or 'good call'. *'I'm thinking I might try the cheesecake.' 'Dreams, man. Dreams.'*

duckface

noun

A face made by pushing the lips forward to accentuate their size, generally utilised by teenage girls in selfies.

The term may also be used to refer to anyone who has had collagen injections, giving them a pouting look.

dudevorce
noun
The split between bros when the bromance is over. See also **bromance**.

dumpster fire
noun
A disaster, something bad that nobody wants to have to deal with: *Did you see Harper's open mic performance the other week? Total dumpster fire.*

dumpster hot
adjective
A person who projects a look of simultaneous trashiness and hotness, wherein their hotness is almost amplified by their trashiness: *Ke$ha is totally dumpster hot.*

e-cig

noun

Electronic cigarette for inhaling vaporised flavoured liquid. Usually containing a combination of nicotine, flavouring and other chemicals, e-cigs are thought to be less harmful than traditional cigarettes and have been used by people as a step towards quitting smoking altogether. See also **vaping**.

Efron

noun

A male who is aesthetically perfect – like an Abercrombie and Fitch model kind of perfect – yet devoid of any and all charisma and talent; filler, a prop, somebody you would take on a date to show off to an ex, but who you would direct, very sternly, not to speak for the duration of whatever you were attending, in order to make your ex jealous.

emoji

noun

A pictorial alphabet used in electronic communication (mostly text messages) to express an object, idea or emotion. There are more than a thousand different emojis, but the two most commonly used are the smiley face (☺) and the sad face (☹).

emoticon

noun

Portmanteau of *emotion* and *icon*; pictorial representations of faces using combinations of letters, numbers and punctuation marks, which has become a staple in digital conversations. The most commonly employed emoticons are those easiest to make using brackets and semi-colons or colons, including happy :), sad :(and winking ;).

environmentally conscious

adjective

To be conscious of the environment; a likely to be used in connection with waste management strategies and conservational activities. *I don't use plastic bags when I go grocery shopping because I am like, totally environmentally conscious.*

extra

noun / adjective

Someone who shouldn't be there, someone expendable who – generally – you don't like: *'Who's that chick over there?' 'I dunno. She's extra.'*

face time
noun
Non-digital human interaction; face-to-face real-world and real-time interactions between people that are not interrupted by a digital screen. So, no, your Skype calls are not considered face time.

Facebook
noun
An online social networking service used for connecting and communicating between people. Mostly mums.

fail
noun
Failure. screw-up, metaphorical car crash, disaster; generally employed in a jovial manner: *38 of the funniest fails by people who are literally the worst.*

fair trade
adjective
A social movement that promotes better international trading conditions for commodity producers and workers in still-developing countries (often Third World nations). Products (most commonly coffee, tea, cocoa and textiles) traded under these guidelines are generally labelled by a certified fair trade body.

false equivalent

noun

An inaccurate analogy employed by a user in order to equate one thing with another where these two ideas are far removed.

fam

abbreviation

Short for *family*, but generally used when addressing or referring to a singular person and not a group of people (so, not an entire family). Doesn't have to be in reference to someone who is actually biologically related to you, just someone with whom you are very close – close enough to consider family: *Benny's my bro, my fam, you feel me?*

fanboy / fangirl

noun

Someone who is passionate about an aspect of nerd and/or geek culture. A male who regularly attends *Star Wars* conventions would be considered a *Star Wars fanboy*.

fap

verb / noun

To masturbate; the sound produced when a male is masturbating.

fat shaming

verb

The act of humiliating or criticising a person in regards to their weight, often justified as a way to motivate people to be thinner: *Hey, bro, I wasn't fat shaming, I was just trying to help that chick get off the couch and lose those two extra pounds.*

feels

noun

A feeling of extreme emotion; a catchall word for the emotionally inarticulate ie, people who use the internet way too much. *I just watched the first ten minutes of* Up. *So many feels.*

fetch

adjective

Cool; originating from the 2004 comedy film *Mean Girls*, a term used by mean girl Gretchen Weiners, who was really trying to make the word take off. Despite mean girl Regina George claiming that *fetch* was never going to happen, for the ironically inclined ,this term has kind of taken off in recent years. Expect to hear fetch on the street in 2017.

finesse

verb

To skilfully manipulate a person or situation; whether it be to smooth over an emotional disagreement between people, or to talk someone out of their belongings: *We'd only been back at my place for 5 minutes before I'd finessed him out of his clothes.*

First World problems

phrase

Minor problems experienced by people who enjoy the social and economic privileges of the First World; may include issues such as being indecisive about which restaurant to eat at, becoming irritated when internet service drops out briefly, or becoming stressed by the fact that you don't have enough leave to cover your entire European vacation. Employed with regard to matters of great triviality when compared to those not living in the First World who have to worry about *real* things. You know, like where their next meal is coming from. See also **#blessed** and **#checkyourprivilege**.

flavourgasm
noun
Portmanteau of *flavour* and *orgasm*; the extreme delight or joy experienced by eating food or being introduced to a particularly good-tasting beverage.

fo shiz / shizzle
phrase
Meaning 'for sure' or 'certainly': *'Is it okay if I help myself to a drink?' 'Fo shizzle my nizzle.'*

FOMO
noun
Acronym of *fear of missing out*: *I can't believe I'm not at that Kanye store launch, my FOMO is super-high right now.*

food miles
noun
The distance that food travels from the place it is produced to get to your plate. Relating to environmentalism, commonly used to highlight the wasted resources and emissions produced in order to transport food very long distances. See also **locavore**.

footprint
noun
The outcome or cost of your existence produced via your accumulated use of resources and waste. Predominantly used in regard to carbon emissions –

your *carbon footprint* – but not the only context in which it can be used. Reducing your footprint is a prerogative among environmentally conscious individuals.

for real
interjection

An exclamation, affirmation, and/or question expressing validity or disbelief. Use is dependent on context, but the possibilities seem endless. Can be shortened to FR, so be aware: *I saw Mr Jones drinking straight vodka. For real.*; *You got 76 likes on that photo of you eating a hard-boiled egg? Are you for real?*

freegan
noun

Portmanteau of *free* and *vegan*; a person who eats only free, discarded food, typically from the refuse of shops or restaurants, supposedly for ecological and/or ethical reasons and nothing to do with them just being tight.

freemium
adjective

A pricing strategy whereby a product or service is provided for free, but money is charged for additional features; usually relating to digital applications such as software and games like *Angry Birds*, *Candy Crush* and *Grindr*.

friend zone
noun

A relationship status between friends whereby one party is sexually attracted to the other, but this feeling is not reciprocated; largely a male creation referring to the inability of a man attracted to a woman to elevate their relationship beyond friendship, and where, after attempting to do so, the man has been told by the woman, 'I just want to be friends'. This experience is sometimes referred to as being *friend zoned*.

Fun Police

noun
Party pooper; someone who just spoils the fun: *I can't believe your dad wouldn't let us wear those Nazi uniforms to Ricki's Halloween party. Who died and made him the Fun Police?*

fungry

adjective
Portmanteau of *f@#king hungry*; to be beyond mere hunger; essentially the equivalent of saying, 'I'm so hungry I could eat a horse', only much more rude and snappy.

furry

noun
A participant in the subculture of people interested in anthropomorphic animal characters. The subculture reached its zenith in mass culture with the help of the internet, allowing participants to connect and organise furry conventions such as Anthrocon, where fans can meet and engage in a range of activities. The conflation of furry fandom with sexual fetishism isn't necessarily an accurate one, though. Like all things born of the

internet, if it can be imagined then it exists, but this isn't the definition we're providing here, nor the one we wish to propagate. See also **Fursona**.

fursona

noun

Portmanteau of *furry* and *persona*; the character, alter ego, avatar, identity or persona assumed by a member of the furry fandom community. See also **furry**.

FYI

phrase

Initialism of *for your information*; can be used when attempting to elucidate a point, but can also be employed when trying to add a little sass: *People don't actually call them 'jorts' anymore, FYI.*

game recognise game
phrase
Acknowledging or recognising someone's achievements and/or abilities; a proverbial doffing of the hat.

game changer
phrase
An event or element that significantly alters the outcome of something: *The addition of sriracha to that mac and cheese was a total game changer.*

Germaneered
verb
The most efficient way to state that something was engineered in Germany, which is kind of like German engineering in itself.

GF
noun
Short for *girlfriend: Me and the GF are ready for Comicpalooza this weekend!* See also **BF**.

ghosting
verb
Leaving a party or event unnoticed and without saying goodbye to anyone.

#GhostRideTheWhip
hashtag

An attachment to a social media post showing the act of putting one's car in neutral while driving slowly, then exiting said car to dance to the loud music playing from within as it rolls forward. (Just look it up on YouTube.)

GIF
noun

Acronym for *Graphics Interchange Format*. (The inventor of the GIF, Steve Wilhite, continues to insist that, despite the first word of the acronym being *graphics*, the correct pronunciation is *JIF*. The rest of the world continues to ignore him.) Essentially just an image format, most commonly used to describe animated GIFs; short, soundless, looped videos that are bizarrely mesmerising.

giving me life
phrase

Energising, invigorating; something that is exciting, fun, uplifting and making you feel good: *The latest season of America's Next Top Redditor is seriously giving me life.*

glamping
noun

Portmanteau of *glamourous* and *camping*; a style of camping that eschews the traditional goals of 'roughing it' and 'getting back to nature' in favour of

bringing along all of the luxuries of home. Also a style of luxury accommodation that resembles camping only in that the walls of your five-star hotel room are made of canvas.

glitter roots
noun
A fashion trend that involves applying gel to the roots of your hair along a part, then sprinkling with glitter. The appropriate accompanying hair-style to this fashion craze is, of course, 'space buns', and if you don't know what they are then just forget it, you're probably so lost at this point in the conversation that it's simply time to give up and walk away. While we hope to remain topical as possible, we hope this trend is long gone before this book even goes to press.

Globalian
noun
A member of the globe, which we all are; an entirely redundant name for a person who calls planet Earth their home.

globalisation
noun
The process of international integration where products, ideas and culture are concerned; rapidly advanced with the advent of instant communication provided by modern technology and the internet.

#goals
hashtag
An attachment to a social media post that depicts or describes something you wish to achieve. Most often

used in relation to fitness #*goals*, beauty #*goals* and squad #*goals*: *Bad bitches SLAYING at the VMAs #goals.* See also **squad**.

Google doodle

noun

An altered, often interactive, version of the logo on Google's homepage; a temporary change designed to commemorate a person, event or special day in the calendar.

gormazing

adjective

Portmanteau of *gorgeous* and *amazing*; an expression of pleasure, whether you're saying 'this food is wonderful' or 'that dress is on fleek'.

grind

noun

Work, effort, slog, hustle; to be busy and doing your best: *Man, I am working 26 hour days, I am really on the grind.*

grip

noun

A lengthy period of time; while not an exact measurement, it does mean 'a lot': *I haven't been home in a grip*; *it took us a grip to finish that run*; *it's been a grip since I played D&D.*

guestimate

noun / verb

Portmanteau of *guess* and *estimate*; the simultaneous process of guessing and estimating: *By my guestimate, we're maybe forty minutes away from our destination.*

# #
prefix

(Or *hashtag*). The hash or pound symbol used to precede a word or series of words with no spaces as part of a social media post. Primarily used as a tag to assist search functionality, the hashtag has since transcended its original purpose and is often used with a more expressive purpose to add context, depth or additional information, or to add a disclaimer.

haters
noun

Anybody (and we're waving our metaphorical index finger in your face as we tell you this), *anybody* who tries to stand in your way. Easily identified by their propensity to hate: *Haters gonna hate, bro, just be yo'self. #YOLO*

hella
prefix

Very, really; emphasises the degree to which something is x or y. If something is *hella cool* then it's 'really cool'. If something was *hella bad* then it was 'very bad'.

hells yeah

interjection

An incredibly obnoxious way of expressing your excitement in the affirmative: *'Wanna go for some froyo?' 'Hells yeah!'*

high key

adjective

When something is of such great importance it needs to be said out loud; can refer to an extreme dislike or something positive that needs to be said. Either way, everybody needs to know. See also **low key.**

hipster

noun

A broad aesthetic and social trend that is marked by irony and nostalgia, where hipster tastes dictate which type of glass your craft beer is served in, and what kind of tattoo your partner is thinking about getting.

hit me up

phrase

To get in touch or make contact with someone for a specific purpose; generally employed as an invitation: *Tell your momma to hit me up on Facebook.* Can also carry negative implications when employed in the past tense: *I got home from work yesterday and my dad hit me up for rent money the second I walked through the door.*

hunty

verb

Portamanteau of *honey* and … well, something insulting beginning with 'c' that we can't print here; originating from popular reality-television show *RuPaul's Drag Race.*

I see what you did there

phrase

Admiration for someone's wit, especially appropriate as an expression of approval with regard to a pun: *'Did you hear about the guy whose whole left side was cut off? He's all right now.' 'I see what you did there.'*

I'm just saying

phrase

Often employed to qualify an opinion, to make the opinion more subtle by obfuscation. The employment of the phrase is largely redundant, as the impact of the user's expressed sentiment is rarely subdued: *'Wow, that movie sucked.' 'I really liked it.' 'Yeah, well, I'm just saying.'*

IDFWU

phrase

Initialism of *I don't f#%K with you*; demonstrates not wanting anything to do with another person, generally due to animosity. Might be employed to signal the end of a relationship: *IDFWU anymore.*

if you will

phrase

Commonly employed by people attempting to sound more intelligent and sophisticated than they actually are. Mostly over-used, although it can be employed to humorous effect ironically, where its use is deliberately exaggerated: *You could say, if you will, that I'm 'in the biz', if you will.*

ignorance is bliss

phrase

Often co-opted by people attempting to justify their apathy regarding a particular subject. Commonly, 'ignorance' is mistakenly used to mean 'deliberately turning a blind eye' and thus shifting the word's original meaning. *I couldn't really say whether we should take in Syrian refugees because I don't really know anything about those dudes. Ignorance is bliss, man #blessed.*

immersive design

noun

Online content, video games and web designs that provide users with an 'immersive' experience, meaning that the users feel engaged and stimulated by the content or program they are using.

impact

noun

Effect, influence: *The work of James Joyce has had a big impact on my career as an author.*

IMO / IMHO

phrase

Initialism of *in my opinion / in my humble opinion*; a common qualifier used to preface a sentence that is clearly an opinion, making it commonly redundant: *IMHO, Johnny Depp's performance in Mortdecai was one of his best. I love that movie.*

Instagram

noun

A photo-sharing social media app, best described as a digital photo album. If you're a selfie-addict then you've got to have an Instagram account.

Instaworthy

adjective

Denoting that something is incredibly visually appealing and also notable, worthy of posting to Instagram: *You look seriously amazeballs great in that dress. The whole look is totes Instaworthy.*

ironic

adjective

Not just a word: a lifestyle. Ironic is to wear Hawaiian shirts. Ironic is to own a VHS player. Ironic is to still be playing your Game Boy. Ironic is chic right now, it's so freaking in it's not even funny. Hey, why not this new word: *ironchic*?

irregardless

adjective

Regardless. *Irregardless* is not a real word; the combination of prefix *ir-* and suffix *-less* work to cancel each other out, meaning that those who employ this term technically say the opposite of what they mean to say.

it's been real

phrase

Signals the end of something; usually used as a farewell before a departure and generally denoting a good experience has been had by the user: *Thanks for standing in for my girlfriend today. It's been real.*

it's complicated

phrase

Conveys that a subject is not open for further discussion; usually used in context with regard to personal matters: *'How are things going between you and Sam after the peanut butter disaster?' 'It's complicated.'*

jackalope
noun
A fictional creature that is a cross between a jackrabbit and an antelope; the subject of many taxidermy attempts that results in a large rabbit with antlers. The creature has been created by taxidermists around the world and pictures of these creations abound online.

jackintosh
noun
Portmanteau of *Macintosh* (the old Apple computer) and *jack off* (meaning, to masturbate): a computer used exclusively for viewing pornography.

jelly
adjective
Short for *jealous*: *Tanya is so jelly of Sid, whose new BF is totes hot.*

JFDI

phrase

Initialism of *just f#%king do it*; the classic Nike slogan with some added punch. If you're ever in need of motivation, just remind yourself: *JFDI*.

JK

phrase

Short for *just kidding*; sometimes employed accompanying text in digital conversation where, due to the absence of tone and inflection, the intention of what is being said may not be clear to the recipient: *Look, I just wish you would die. JK!*

Juggalo

noun

A fan of American hip-hop duo Insane Clown Posse (or ICP), a rap group that comprises the wicked clowns known as Violent J and Shaggy 2 Dope. Together the ICP perform a style of hardcore hip-hop music known as 'horrorcore'. These fans dress in terrifying clown attire and are known for being cult-like and obsessive.

Kardashian

noun

A person who displays the unflattering character traits most associated with the Kardashian family; someone who is vacuous and lacks any discernible skills.

keep it

phrase

Indicates approval: *Honey, your crop top is bomb. Keep it.*

killed it

phrase

To have unambiguously succeeded.

kombucha

noun

Fermented, lightly effervescent sweetened tea drink known for its alleged probiotic health benefits. Made by hipsters who subscribe to the 'wellness' movement, in giant jars full of murky brown liquid topped with bacteria sludge.

legit
adjective
Abbreviation of *legitimate*; valid, sound or well founded.
Used when referencing something absolute, but can
be employed as a statement of opinion: *The burgers at
McDonald's are legit.*

let my girls hang
phrase
Not wearing a bra; generally associated with the sweet
relief of removing your bra: *I can't wait to get home and let
my girls hang.*

levelution
noun
Portmanteau of *level* and *evolution*; the process of
increasing in popularity. As someone or something
becomes more famous or popular, they progressively
level up: *In recent years, movie-goers have witnessed the
levelution of Jennifer Lawrence.*

life
noun
Amazing, the most incredible thing in your existence at
the present time: *Dude, this chocolate cake is life.* See also
giving me life.

life changing

phrase

Any experience or event that elicits extreme emotions: *That seminar was life changing.*

life hack

noun

A short-cut or work-around; a tool, system or idea that you can employ to make a task simpler. Popular website *Buzzfeed* publishes regular articles on the topic, using a grapefruit and salt to polish glass, paying someone to queue for you when you don't have the time to wait, and blowing into your game cartridge when your Nintendo 64 won't load up properly.

lifestyle vlogger

noun

A person who records and publishes regular videos (generally on YouTube) portraying the minutiae of their daily life. These videos are usually aspirational and somewhat instructional, with a specific focus on health, fashion or beauty. Lifestyle vlogs are particularly popular in the fitness community, where vloggers share their diet and exercise routines.

like

conjunction

Employed as a way to stall for emphasis; an in-sentence pause. Can also be used deliberately and ironically, where its employment to exaggeratedly break the flow of a sentence or thought affects vagueness or sassiness or stupidity: *We were all just, like, hanging out until, like, Mark came along and just, like, went crazy for, like, no reason at all.* Or: *Like, hello? Are you, like, stupid or something?*

listicle

noun

Portmanteau of *list* and *article*; an article (usually published online, but the style has expanded to print) presented in the form of a list. The headlines of these articles usually include the number of items in the list, such as, '16 Olympians Who Are Really, Really Ridiculously Good Looking' or '73 Acid-Wash Jumpsuits You Need Right Now'. See also ***BuzzFeed***.

lit

adjective

Awesome, excellent; used when you need to express how great something was. Can also be used to mean something 'went off', and can also mean that someone is drunk, especially if their subsequent behaviour is outlandish: *I heard that party the other week was lit.* Or: *Check this guy out; dude is lit.*

literally

adverb

Figuratively. Yes, this words now means the opposite of what it, literally, means. An amplifier used to emphasis the impact of information, especially when the statement is clearly exaggerated: *Missing out on the last copy of Kim Kardashian's book is literally the worst thing to happen to anyone, ever.*

live

adjective

Exciting, cool, awesome, amazing; can also imply that this same thing was intense or extreme in some way: *'How was Jayden's fondue party last night?' 'Oh, man, it was seriously live.'*

localisation
noun
A market term that refers to the desires of modern consumers for products that are local and ideally, independent. Has contributed to the rise in popularity of craft beer and reflects current importance being placed on locally-sourced food produce. See also **food miles**, **locavore**.

locavore
noun
A person who eats only local produce, usually food grown and raised within a certain radius from where they live.

lols / lulz
noun
Fun, laughter, amusement; originating from *LOL*, the acronym for *laughing out loud*. *'Did you see what Britney was wearing on the red carpet? She really brought the lolz there!'*

lose–lose situation
phrase
A scenario whereby, no matter what happens, the outcome will be negative. Generally implies that you have to make a choice between two or more options, and all choices will lead to a negative result. See also **win–win**.

low key
phrase
A secret, something that cannot be stated out loud; basically a new way of saying on the down low. See also **DL**, **high key**.

lumbersexual

noun / adjective

Portmanteau of *lumberjack* and *metrosexual*; an urban male identified by a dress code that includes a heavy beard, work boots and a checked shirt, drawing influence from the aesthetic of wood-cutting professionals. A style that promotes an air of ruggedness and implies an active outdoor lifestyle, in reality most adherents are city-dwellers who wouldn't know which end of the hand-crafted artisanal axe they have hanging above their bed is used for splitting wood.

man bun

noun

An ugly, ugly tuft of hair positioned atop a male head and tied into a small bun – this be a man bun, hon. If your BF is rocking one, it's time to step out.

Manic Pixie Dream Girl / MPDG

noun

A cinema term and character type, first identified by American film critic Nathan Rabin. The *MPDG* is depicted as vivacious and appealingly quirky, whose main purpose within the film's narrative is to inspire a greater appreciation for life in a male protagonist. Examples include: Claire from *Elizabethtown* (Kirsten Dunst), Sam from *Garden State* (Natalie Portman) and Summer Finn in *500 Days of Summer* (Zooey Deschanel).

mansplaining

verb

Portmanteau of *man* and *explaining*; the act of a man speaking in a condescending manner to someone (typically, a woman) with the incorrect assumption that he knows more about the subject at hand than the person he is talking to: *My dad totally mansplained menstruation to me last night.*

manspreading
verb

The action of a male taking up a large amount of space in a shared or public area (such as public transport), most commonly by sitting with legs spread wide apart, with no regard to the inconvenience and discomfort caused to those around him.

marketability
noun

The degree to which something is able to be marketed towards a general audience or specific demographic: *We were going to put Lindsay Lohan in our ad campaign, but she's got no marketability anymore.*

Marvel Cinematic Universe (MCU)
noun

A cinematic franchise of films produced by Marvel Studios, based on Marvel comics, all set in the same fictional space. Movies set within the *MCU* include *Iron Man*, *Thor*, *Captain America* and *The Avengers*, so basically every movie that has come out in the past few years and every movie that will be released in the forseeable future.

McConaissance
noun

Portmanteau of *McConaughey* and *renaissance*; the late-career success of actor Matthew McConaughey since the early 2010s. Having made a career in Hollywood films predominantly as a romantic lead since 1992, McConaughey's star power had been steadily dwindling before his resurgence in popularity thanks to highly-acclaimed performances in a succession of celebrated films, including *Mud*, *Magic Mike*, *Dallas Buyer's Club* (for which McConaughey received an Academy Award) and *Interstellar*, as well as the hit TV series *True Detective*.

megaphone
noun
The jerk talking too loudly on his cell or mobile phone: t*hat guy just won't shut up, what a megaphone douche of the highest order.*

meh
interjection / adjective
A verbal shrug; expresses indifference. Can be used as a response to a question: *'What did you think of Thor 17?' 'Meh.'* Or as description: *I liked the performances in Monopoly: The Movie, but the costumes were kind of meh.*

meme
noun
An image, video or piece of text that is usually humorous in nature and is copied and spread rapidly by internet users. Memes may appear with slight variations.

memephobia
noun
The fear that something will go viral, just like a meme; a concern that the picture or video someone snapped

of you in a compromising or humiliating situation may find a global audience. Ain't nobody got time for that! See also **viral**.

mic drop

verb

The literal or metaphorical deliberate act of dropping a microphone after delivering an amazing performance, where this action serves to punctuate said performance. After delivering information that is revolutionary and/or awe-inspiring in some way,

one may feign the act of dropping a microphone, or just say '*mic drop*' before leaving the conversation or stage.

microbrew

noun

A craft beer. The abundance of microbreweries popping up all over the world gives hipsters one more thing to claim to have been into before everybody else.

millennial

noun

A person who reached a stage of adolescence or young adulthood around the year 2000; also known as generation Y. There is no official demarcation of the much-derided millennial generation, but it is generally thought to be those born between the early 1980s and mid-1990s. If you'd like to blame anyone for being lazy, entitled and causing terrorism and sky-rocketing house prices, millennials should be your go to.

'mirin
verb
Short for *admiring*; often written without the apostrophe simply as *mirin*: *Hey, baby, you 'mirin me? Because I can see you lookin'.*

moblivious
adjective
Portmanteau of *mobile* and *oblivious*; lack of awareness that results from staring at a mobile phone screen: *Those damn pesky kids not looking where they're going are completely moblivious to their surroundings!*

mukbang
noun
A video of someone eating; specifically, a form of online content that was popularised in South Korea during the early 2010s, whereby a 'host' eats large quantities of food while interacting with their audience via chatrooms.

MVP
noun
Initialism of *most valuable player*; and is generally used in a sporting context, whereby awards given at the end of a season may include the MVP trophy. However, MVP can also be employed in day-to-day speak to refer to someone whose work or contribution or personality you deem valuable.

Mx
pronoun
A gender neutral and/or queer formal pronoun that replaces other formal pronouns such as Ms, Mrs or Mr.

nailed it
phrase
To unequivocally succeed at something; to get a perfect result. Can be employed ironically to mean the opposite, indicating a humorous failure: *My rainbow layer cupcakes came out looking like lumpy brown potatoes. Nailed it.*

neg
noun
A negative comment primarily intended to make someone feel bad, but most commonly employed as a pick-up technique that deliberately undermines confidence in a way that makes a person more receptive to advances. This action is referred to as *negging*.

nerdgasm
noun
Portmanteau of *nerd* and *orgasm*; the extreme excitement expressed by a nerd over something nerdy: *When Jason watched The Flash for the first time, he had a total nerdgasm over how fast Barry Allen could run.*

Netflix and chill
phrase
The act of relaxing and watching programs via the media streaming service Netflix, often with company.

Also used in online dating circles as a euphemism for a one-night stand: *Hey, you want to come over to mine for Netflix and chill?*

neuromorphics

noun

Building and training computers to think like human beings. While the concept has been around a long time, the term only started to gain traction in 2014 when *The Huffington Post* declared it the biggest buzzword of that year. Its absence from common language today speaks to the failure of this word to take off among members of the public, but we feel this is still worth noting.

newsjacking

verb

Portmanteau of *news* and *highjacking*; exploiting a breaking news story in order to advertise or promote a brand or product.

next level

phrase

Elevated in quality; if the burger you just ate or the song you recently heard is *next level* then that burger or that song is, respectively, a better burger or song than the majority of other burgers or songs: *Have you heard Kanye's latest album? That is some next level sh*t.*

nocialise

verb

Portmanteau of *no* and *socialise*; anti-social behaviour affected via the use of modern technology, such as ignoring people in favour of playing Angry Birds. See also **phubbing**.

normcore

noun / adjective

A fashion style characterised by the elevation of bland, 'normal' clothing, with the intention of positioning the wearer as conspicuously unpretentious. The very fact of its existence and its (ambiguously ironic) popularity with hipsters has turned the style into a trend, making its claim of being unpretentious decidedly pretentious. Normcore is also associated with the revival of 1990s-era clothing which has led to all of the cool kids dressing like George Costanza in an attempt to go unnoticed, but with a hidden agenda: to be seen and to be adored.

NSFW

adjective

Initialism of *not safe for work*; used in a link or email subject line to warn that 'adult' content lies beyond, something you don't want displayed on your computer screen should you manager happen to walk past.

'nuff said

phrase

Short for *enough said*; a full stop of sorts, saying 'you needn't say anymore' and 'message received': *Michael Jordan was the greatest basketball player to ever put on a jersey. 'Nuff said.*

obvi

adjective

Short for *obvious* or *obviously*; reached popularity through the hit teen drama show *The OC* back in the mid-2000s. And yet it has somehow made a resurgence lately. *Obvi* is back! *Obvi* is best served with a side of eye roll. Those who want to get their sass on need only employ this word in place of 'duh'.

OG

noun

Initialism of *original gangster.* Originating from gangsta rap, the term has found broad use as a synonym for 'original', with nostalgic connotations: *Paris Hilton was totally the OG reality queen. Kim Kardashian would be nothing if it weren't for Paris.* See also **old school**.

old school

adjective

Old fashioned, but often used with an implication of respect and deference; may be employed with regard to a person, place, thing or action. If someone is described as being old school then they conjure sensibilities associated with past eras: *That gramophone is seriously old school. Wish I had one to listen to the new Skrillex album on. Oh, it's just for decoration? Cool.*

on blast
phrase

To draw attention to a person or thing in a critical manner: *Sorry, Diane, but I'm going to have to put you on blast right now. That was totally not cool.*

on fleek
adjective

Perfectly executed, on point; apparently originally used to describe immaculate eyebrows, but nobody seems to know where this really came from or what it means, other than it being a expression of high praise: *Cara Delevingne's eyebrows are on fleek.*

on point
adjective

Perfection, exactness, highly suitable; used to state that something is of excellent quality: *that slice of za was seriously on point.*

one-hundo per cent
phrase

Short for one-hundred per cent; most commonly used to signify absolute certainty: *'You sure about that, Mike?' 'One-hundo per cent, my friend.'*

one-hundred-and-ten per cent
phrase

To exert maximum effort; implying that you are trying so hard that you are somehow exerting even more effort

than the possible limit; to go above and beyond: *Look,
I gave one-hundred-and-ten per cent at the Ultimate Frisbee
championship finals and we still didn't win. I think that it's time
for me to retire.*

Or nah?
phrase
When used at the end of a sentence is employed as a
clarification. It translates most directly as 'is this or is
this not so?': *Are you going to that party tonight, or nah?*

origin story
noun
How a person or thing came to be in the present
moment. Most commonly used in reference to comic
books and films, especially with regard to superheroes,
the origin story can often be both an interesting piece
of backstory and a worn out re-tread over something
many of us familiar with popular culture have already
heard before. *Everyone knows Batman's origin story is that his
mother and father were murdered in an alley. Move on already!*

othering
verb
The marginalising of a person or group of people in
a way that positions them as different to a presumed
'normal'; to make a person feel alien and/or to treat
them as such.

OTP
phrase
Initialism of *one true pairing*; refers to a couple whose
relationship you are emotionally invested in, whose
break-up would pain you. This couple may be people

you know personally, but most commonly your *OTP* are a celebrity couple you've never met, and the phrase is meant semi-ironically. For example: Your OTP might be Kanye and Kim, Beyonce and Jay-Z or maybe Michael Fassbender and Alicia Vikander.

own
verb

To dominate, to aggressively and decisively take victory over something or someone. Alternatively it can be used in the inverse to describe someone or something *getting owned*: *Taylor Swift got completely owned by Kim and Kanye* or *'How did you go with your presentation?' 'I totally owned it!'*

oxygen thief
noun

A person so worthless that the purpose of their existence seems solely to deprive those around them of vital oxygen.

pansexual
noun
A person whose sexual orientation is non-specific and not limited; attracted to people of any sex or gender.

paper
noun
Money, cash, dolla dolla bills: *I'm heading into work, because I gotta make that paper.*

parkour
noun
Also known as *free running*, a form of movement that reimagines urban spaces so that practitioners can navigate their environment, without assistive equipment, in the most efficient and fastest way possible. A training discipline and form of exercise, which originated in France in the 1980s. While utterly impractical, parkour does look pretty cool and the techniques are often employed in action sequences in TV commercials and Hollywood films.

part the kimono
phrase
To reveal an aspect of life; used when demonstrating something previously unknown or not apparent to a

person or peoples with regard to something (similar to 'to lift the curtain'): *You want to know how this all works? Let me part the kimono a little for you.*

PAW
phrase

Initialism of *parents are watching*; a warning to whoever you are in communication with online, letting them know that your parents are around and that you might be being monitored, therefore the tone and content need to stay parent friendly. See also **NSFW**.

PC
adjective

(No, it's not the opposite of a Mac.) Initialism of *politically correct*; speech, policies or actions carefully designed to offend no one; the new fundamentalism of our time: *They're serving sushi in the cafeteria again! That is cultural appropriation and just so not PC!*

peacocking
verb

When a human male dresses flamboyantly in order to draw attention from the opposite sex, like a peacock displaying its vibrant plumage.

peeps
noun

Short for *people*; commonly used in the possessive context to indicate a group you might be affiliated with, whether it be your family, your friends, a sports team or social interest group: *I'm catching up with my Hufflepuff peeps later to learn how to make butterbeer.*

photobomb
verb

The act of intruding in a photograph, usually by deliberately disrupting the picture being taken or by standing in the background. While the intention is generally to spoil the outcome, if an

awesome animal should inadvertantly *photobomb* you, then the resulting image is internet gold.

phubbing
verb

Portmanteau of *phone* and *snub*; to ignore your companion(s) and instead direct your attention towards your phone or mobile device.

pimptastic
adjective

Portmanteau of *pimp* and *fantastic*; something that is very pimp, where pimp means bold or ostentatious: *Did you see Jerry's powder-blue metallic hi-tops? They're pimptastic!'*

planking
verb

A mind-bogglingly idiotic trend that involved people lying in highly unusual or compromising situations with their bodies held stiff (like a plank of wood). A photograph of the act would then be uploaded to the internet for millions to see. The only upside of this internet craze was the frightening amount of people who hurt themselves in pursuit of this moronic activity.

playa

noun

A person who is manipulative when it comes to sex and romantic relationships, known to lead their partner/s on in pursuit of their own selfish gains, with no thought given to hurting anyone's feelings: *I can't believe Cherry slept with Miranda an hour after telling Brandon she loved him – she is such a playa.*

podcast

noun

An audio broadcast, usually episodic, that listeners generally subscribe to via apps on their mobile devices. Essentially radio for the digital age: *I've started my own podcast – it's basically me turning the day's* Buzzfeed *articles into spoken-word poetry. You should subscribe on iTunes!*

Pokémon Go

noun

A location-based mobile app game that utilises augmented reality and has captured the hearts and imagination of the contemporary everyman with its perfect blend of nostalgia, idiocy and time-killing behaviour that makes the game so addictive. Haven't downloaded it yet? Then, if you value your time and productivity, don't, we implore you.

PortmanNO

noun

A modern portmanteau word that you find so particularly idiotic and intellectually offensive that you literally can't even. This dictionary is filled with *portmanNOs*, including *phubbing*, *listicle* and *nocialise*.

post

noun

Publication of material online; an upload of content to the internet, commonly associated with blogs or social media: *Have you seen Sharon's latest Facebook post? I'm so jelly of her Bali holiday.*

power couple

phrase

The coupling of two powerful individuals, where that power can be economic, cultural, political, intellectual or otherwise: *Beyonce and Jay Z are music's greatest power couple.*

preach

interjection

An encouraging affirmation: *'Jessica Alba is a stone cold fox.' 'Preach!'*

q-gasm
noun
An orgasm experienced after sticking a q-tip into your ear.

QFT
phrase
Initialism of *quoted for truth*; commonly used on internet forums where its employment is used to, generally, agree with another forum user.

QT
noun
Short for *cutie*: *What's up, QT?*

queen bee
noun
A female 'alpha' or 'leader of the pack'. Usually a term reserved for high schoolers: *The queen bee showed up late to the party in order to make an entrance.*

question fart
noun
Passing wind where the sound ends in an upward inflection, similar to the inflection you would use when asking a question.

quickie

noun

Sexual intercourse performed in a timely manner.

quinoa

noun

An ancient grain bought in organic and/or health food stores by middle-class hipsters.

quirper

noun

A creepy, creepy adult male human who derives sexual pleasure from sniffing bicycle seats, especially those ridden by women.

quizzle

noun

Question: *'Can I ask you a quizzle?' 'Fo shizzle my nizzle.'*
See also **fo shizzle.**

ratchet
adjective
Alternate spelling of *wretched*; originally a derogatory term for a woman perceived as obnoxious and trashy, but now has a broader use describing anything broken or dysfunctional: *My chain came off, this bike is ratchet!*

reach out
phrase
To make contact by any available means; the phrase has grandiose connotations, as though the person making contact believes they are doing you an enormous favour by bestowing their attention on you: *I had to reach out to William to discuss what he's wearing to my party, so I gave him a call.*

read
verb
To point out someone's flaws in a sassy, witty and accurate manner; can be delivered in a humorous manner, kind of like a roast.

reality check
phrase
Employed with the intention of bringing a person into the life of those around them, to ground them or to

bring them back to 'reality'. Can also be used with the intention of attacking someone's aspirations, whereby the reality check forces them to consider the state of their hopes and/or desires and subsequently lower their standards. *'I'm thinking about becoming an astronaut.' 'Reality check, dog, you need to be good at, like, physics and stuff, and you stink at maths.'*

reboot
verb / noun
Most commonly used in relation to the resurrection of a dormant Hollywood film property or franchise, whereby the original film is remade with a different cast, as opposed to continuing the story with a sequel. *I can't wait for the all-male reboot of* The Sisterhood of the Travelling Pants*!*

Reddit
noun
An online entertainment and news aggregator. If you've ever seen someone at work killing time looking at GIFs of cute kittens or reading through countless text scrolls of forum postings dispensing awful relationship advice, chances are they're killing time on Reddit.

rekt
verb
Alternative spelling of *wrecked*; something or someone who has in some way been hurt or humiliated: *Suzanne tried parkour, but then she face-planted and totally rekt herself.*

relatability
adjective
The degree to which something is or is not relatable
either to a mass audience or specific demographic. A
person's *relatability* is their ability for others to identify
with them.

resonate
verb
To evoke a shared feeling; usually the way an event,
subject or persona is accepted by an audience.
Essentially, resonate has come to replace the word
'relate'. If someone or something resonates with others
then it 'goes over well': *Actor Chris Pratt really resonates with
today's young audiences.*

respek
noun
Respect; to give something the respect it deserves and/
or is due. When you put *respek* on someone's name you
draw attention to them in the positive.

responsive web design
noun
Code that allows websites to adapt the way it displays
depending on the size of window and type of device it's
viewed on.

rich media
noun
A term used to describe interactive elements of web
design, usually used to refer to advertising such as
banner advert on a website that expands when you click
on it, or the Google doodle.

ROFL

verb

Acronym for *rolling on floor laughing*; employed when something is so completely and unbelievably funny that a good old simple, classic LOL just does not suffice to express the extreme hilarity being experienced.

RT

verb

Short for *retweet*, which is a function of the social media platform Twitter where you post someone else's tweet into your feed thus sharing it with your followers.

sadiculous

adjective

Portmanteau of *sad* and *ridiculous*; conveys that
something is very sad – ridiculously so. This word is
generally employed where the meaning of sad is closer
to pathetic: *He was trying so hard to dance like Psy, it was
unbelievably sadiculous.*

safe space

noun

A place where someone feels safe from harassment,
or from being exposed to views that may contradict
their own. Largely a phenomenon within educational
institutions, safe spaces are designed to stifle free speech
and emotional maturity.

salty

adjective

Irritated, angry: *After lining up for four hours and missing out
on the last cronut, I'm a little salty right now.*

sarcaustic

adjective

Portmanteau of *sarcastic* and *caustic*; a tone of scathing
irony used to convey contempt.

savage

adjective

Cool in a sassy kind of way: *RuPaul is so savage, she throws the best shade.*

screen rage

noun

Anger that is directed at a screen. If you've ever blown up at your iPhone while playing a game of *Candy Crush* then you've experienced *screen rage.*

selfie

noun

A photograph of you, taken by you; popularised by social media where it is very common for users to post endless pictures of themselves.

selfie stick

noun

An extensible metal stick used to position a camera or phone beyond the length of one's arm in order to take selfie photographs. Generally acknowledged to be one of the harbingers of the apocalypse. See also **selfie**.

seriously

adverb

An indicator that you mean something in earnest; *I am seriously dying to get out of this room. Seriously, it's so damn seriously hot in here.*

sext

noun / verb

A text message of a sexually explicit nature; can be text, or a photograph. *Sext* can refer to the message itself, or the act of sending the message: *I'm totally going to sext Brian this pic of my boobs.*

sharing economy

noun

An economic system in which assets or services are shared between private individuals either for free or for a fee, typically facilitated by the internet. Companies such as Airbnb and Uber are based on this system.

ship

verb

Short for *relationship*; the projected desire for a relationship to occur between two people, fictional or otherwise. Employed by fans of the two people who want to see them together. *I am totally shipping John Snow and Daenerys. I ship them so hard. It just makes so much sense, you know?*

shoutout

noun / verb

A public acknowledgement; to mention someone publicly in a positive manner: *When accepting my award I gave a shoutout to my pops.*

sickening

adjective

Causing a level of discomfort via overwhelming levels of something normally perceived as positive: *God, Channing Tatum is so attractive it's sickening. I literally can't even.*

Siri

noun

A voice-controlled intelligent personal assistant computer program created by Apple Inc.; can be used as an insult to describe someone you consider a 'know-it-all', or an affectionate term for someone who always has a handy answer up their sleeve.

siriris

noun

Alternative term for *palindrome*; also an acronym for *spelled in reverse it remarkably is same*. Has the advantage over palindrome in that it demonstrates the quality it describes; has the disadvantage of being a bit stupid.

sis

noun

Short for *sister*; can describe your biological sister, but more commonly employed to a member of your squad; your bestie, your homie, the girl you take all those selfies with. See also **BFF**.

Skrillex

noun

An American electronic 'musician' known predominantly for popularising a form of 'music' known as dub-step; the creator of unending streams of context-less noise likely to deafen you and cause blood to pour from your ears.

slay

verb

To succeed, in a way that suggests any competitors have been annihilated; to dominate: *Kanye's new album slays*.

SMH

phrase

Initialism of *shaking my head*, SMH is an abbreviation used to convey that the user finds something so stupid that they can't find the words to relate this feeling. *'I've never been knocked out before, so I deliberately smashed my head against a wall to see what it would be like.' 'What happened?' 'Nothing. I just got a massive bump on my head.' 'SMH.'*

smize

verb

To smile using only your eyes; a modelling technique coined by model and host of *America's Next Top Model* Tyra Banks.

snatched

adjective

Flawless, on point. If you're outfit is tight, it's *snatched*. If you're slayin' in your cocktail dress, you're *snatched*. See also **on fleek**.

social justice warrior (SJW)

noun

A combative personality whose extroverted and vocal desire for social justice (expressed predominantly online) is perceived as annoying and deliberately antagonistic (and generally completely ineffectual). Typically a white, middle-class university graduate whose extremist left-wing politics are a result of having experienced no adversity and a high level of privilege. Generally attempts to affect social change via hurling abuse at people on Twitter.

social media

noun

Computer-mediated websites and tools that allow individuals and organisations to exchange information and visual content within online networks. Facebook, Instagram, Twitter are all social media platforms.

sorry, not sorry

phrase

Indicates that you are sorry that a person disagrees with you, but that you will happily ignore the difference in opinion and proceed in the way you intended; an apology for the fact that you are not, in fact, sorry at all.

spoiler alert

noun

A statement that must accompany any review or comment regarding a movie, TV show or video game, warning the reader that plot points are going to be revealed. Failure to do so, and the subsequent 'spoiling' that occurs will bring the wrath of the entire internet down upon your head.

squad

noun

You crew or posse; in plain English, it means 'group of friends'.

stan

noun

Portmanteau of *stalker* and *fan*; you don't want no *stans* in your world, trust us – listen to the hit Eminem song *Stan*. You'll get the idea.

starchitect

noun

Portmanteau of *star* and *architect*; any world-famous architect whose aesthetic style and creations are awe-inspiring, aka, the three architects you've ever heard of: *Frank Lloyd Wright, Frank Gehry and Le Corbusier are total starchitects —I respect their work so much.*

startup

noun

A newly formed company whose business model generally relies on or is related to innovative technologies and the internet. Startup companies are often created and run (and run into the ground) by millennials, though not always.

staycation

noun

A vacation in which you stay at home for the duration (not literally inside your home, but in your home area); leisure time that does not involve travelling long distances. A chance for a vacationer to enjoy the comforts of home and to develop an appreciation for the offerings of your home environ.

streaming

verb

A method of accessing content via the internet as a flow of data, without having to download it first. Additionally, *live streaming* refers to the broadcast and consumption of various media online in real time: *Darren is live streaming baby Jaxon's first nappy change! I've gotta get home and watch it!*

suh
interjection
Portmanteau of *sup* (the abbreviation of *wassup*) and *huh*;
an exclamation of excitement and confusion: *'Hey, man.'*
'Suh, dude.'

sus
adjective
Short for *suspect* or *suspicious*; shady situations or people
whose words or actions aren't earning your trust: *I don't
know about Brayden. Dude seems kinda sus to me.*

swag
adjective
Short for *swagger*; an expression of exterior confidence.
A way of carrying yourself that suggests impressiveness,
a look that exudes style, certainty and success: *Kanye
has swag. Kanye has swag in abundance. Kanye has seventeen
truckloads of swag.*

synergy
noun
Combining forces for greater productivity and mutual
understanding, aka, *the* marketing buzzword of a couple
of years ago, aka, utterly meaningless.

TBH

phrase

Initialism of *to be honest*; a redundant and overused phrase employed by the inarticulate when attempting to cement a point: *I didn't like that movie at all, TBH.*

tea

noun

Gossip; presumably originating due to tea and gossip generally being consumed together in homes and workplaces around the world. If you're hanging onto some good *tea*, it may be time to spill it.

terrarium

noun

A cute glass globe or similar-shaped container in which rocks, plants and sometimes adorable tiny figurines are placed for display. Popular among hipsters.

TGIF

phrase

Initialism of *thank God it's Friday*, used to express feeling relief or pleasure that the interminable grind of working week is finally, finally at its end and you have two blissful days of weekend ahead of you. Or something like that. *No work for the next two days! TGIF!*

thirsty

adjective

Desperate, trying too hard to get attention, so eager it hurts; experiencing and exhibiting extreme thirst for fame: *Did you see Iggy on* Celebrity Dog Washing *last night? Girl is thirsty AF.*

throwing shade

verb

The act of subtly and wittily insulting someone; an underhand comment or backhanded compliment; bitchiness personified. Throwing shade is something the drag community have been doing for years, and so have you – you just didn't know it had a name. Here's some shade you might like to throw: 'You're so confident. I just love how you don't even care what you look like.'

time sink

noun

Something pointless into which you invest your time and subsequently lose it with no discernable outcome to show for the time spent: *That trip to the froyo store was a total time sink, they didn't even have any of the salted-caramel bacon cronut flavour left.*

tl;dr

phrase

Initialism of *too long; didn't read*; conveys the dismissal of a piece of writing considered to be excessively and/or unnecessarily long. So, basically anything that is longer than two paragraphs: *I was going to buy this book at the store, but the blurb on the back just went on and on and on, so tl;dr.*

tooch

verb

To *tooch* your booty is to pop your derrière out while having your photograph taken, in order to accentuate your rump, making it appear larger, and more plump and round. A modelling technique created by model and host of *America's Next Top Model* Tyra Banks. See also **smize**.

tote bag

noun

The modern replacement for plastic bags, which were deemed icky for the environment – you know, with global warming and all that shiz; a reusable shopping bag that an environmentally conscious person would take to go grocery shopping in places like Whole Foods. See also **environmentally conscious**.

totes

adverb

Abbreviation of *totally*; adds mega-beef to your word game. For example, *totes good* (totally good) *totes adorbs* (totally adorable), *totes appropes* (totally appropriate), *totes inappropes* (totally inappropriate), and *totes magotes* (your guess is as good as ours). Can be employed in almost any situation. Totes ain't going anywhere soon, so just embrace it.

trainwreck

noun

An unmitigated catastrophe or complete and total disaster: *Emily has been a trainwreck ever since she broke up with Ethan.* Or: *That movie was a complete trainwreck from start to finish.*

trans

adjective

Short for *transgender*; a person whose gender identity does not match the biological sex they were born with.

transparency

noun

A corporate strategy buzzword where the word retains most of its traditional meaning, but refers to a company allowing the public to see their inner workings (or at least the version of their inner workings their PR department wants the public to see) in order to seem more trustworthy.

trash

adjective

Anything that's just completely terrible (and hence would be better off being thrown away like garbage): *I hate taking the bus to work. Buses are trash.*

trigger warning

noun

Originally a term used by mental health professionals in relation to patients suffering from PTSD. Soldiers who had witnessed and survived the atrocities of war were sometimes 'triggered' by events in the present – say a hand touching their shoulder unexpectedly – that might cause a flashback or an anxiety attack. Trigger warnings were put in place to avoid this discomfort. Today, the term has been co-opted by college students to help them avoid having to read texts they may find disagreeable: *We must alert the students that Virginia Woolf's* Mrs Dalloway *contains many long-winded descriptions, which may trigger boredom.*

troll

noun

A person who intentionally sows discord on the internet by starting arguments and upsetting people. This is achieved by posting inflammatory, extraneous or off-topic messages in comment sections and on social media and forums with the deliberate intent of provoking emotional responses from other users for the troll's own amusement. Essentially, everything that's bad about the internet.

true that

interjection

A term of agreement meaning 'that's right' or 'yup':
'You know Grayson's girlfriend has no class, right?' 'True that.'

Trumpmentum

noun

Portmanteau of *Trump* and *momentum*; Donald Trump's political momentum while vying for presidency in the 2016 United States election.

#TryLife

hashtag

An attachment to a social media post that promotes motivation for leading a positive lifestyle. Best used in conjunction with an obnoxious motivational phrase such as, 'Today is a great day to have a great day', or, 'Sometimes the smallest decision can change your life forever'.

turducken

noun

A culinary term referring to a roast dish consisting of a chicken stuffed inside a duck stuffed inside a turkey.

turnt

adjective

Amplified, intense; can refer to both a state of inebriation and/or being hyped up: *I was super turnt last night.* Or: *This party is totally turnt.*

twerk

verb

A dance move, most commonly performed by females, that involves a low squatting stance accompanied by ferocious hip-thrusting motions. This century's answer to the Charleston.

u
pronoun

Shorthand for the word 'you', commonly used in digital communications: *C u later.*

U mad bro?
phrase

A redundant question deployed when you are aware that someone is mad, and wish to make them madder.

UDI
noun

Acronym for *unidentified drinking injury*. Damage incurred to your body when so innebriated, you have no memory of it happening.

unboxing
verb

The act of removing a product from its packaging. Videos showing people carrying out this act, especially with Apple products, are insanely, bizarrely popular on YouTube.

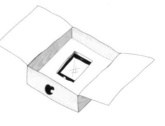

unspun

adjective

Lacking in spin, genuine, authentic; commonly used in political discourse: *The voters are seriously desperate out for some unspun politics.*

upvote

verb

The act of giving online content such as an article, video or forum post a positive rating. For instance, hitting the thumbs-up button or the 'like' button on a YouTube video is to give that video an upvote.

ur

contraction

Short for both *your* and *you're*, which makes this abbreviation a rather irritating one for those insistent on preserving the English language.

v
adverb
Short for very: *I just really don't think Ron is a v good influence on Hermione.*

vaping
verb
Inhaling vapour from an electronic cigarette or vape pen; analogous to smoking, but where the substance inhaled and exhaled is vapour, not smoke.

vaporwave
noun
A music and art genre that emerged in the early 2010s out of genres such as seapunk, bounce house, witch house and chillwave. Vaporwave is characterised by a fascination with nostalgic and surrealist retro cultural aesthetics and styles.

victim blaming / shaming
verb
The act of bringing shame or blame upon someone who is a victim (as opposed to blaming their attacker)

in a way that implies the victim deserved or somehow caused their attack, by way of harassment, usually in a verbal and/or online context.

video on demand (VOD)

noun
Media distribution systems that allow consumers to select when they engage with content rather than being limited to specific broadcast times.

viewability

adjective
The degree to which something is able to be seen or watched or looked at by a mass audience or specific demographic, incorporating also the degree to which that audience will find the visual content stimulating and/or agreeable.

Vine

noun
The name of a social network and of the 5–10 second videos posted to it: *You've gotta check out Kimberly's vine of her hacking that vine on Vine.*

viral

adjective
Content that explodes in popularity and reaches a mass audience within a very short time period. The Holy Grail for digital marketers: *All we need for this campaign to succeed is for it to go viral. Creative, get working on a viral video.*

---

wake 'n bake
phrase

To wake up and smoke marijuana. *Bake* is a derivative of the word *baked*, which is slang for stoned or high in reference to a person intoxicated via the consumption of marijuana. The phrasing is a reference to a breadcrumb-style food product called Shake 'n Bake.

#WCW
hashtag

Acronym for *Woman (or Women) Crush Wednesday*; an attachment to a social media post, published on a Wednesday, about a woman you have a non-romantic crush on, generally with the intention to highlight and celebrate her impressive achievements.

weeaboo
noun

A Japanophile; a non-Japanese person who is obsessed with Japan and Japanese culture and who has adopted and incorporated parts of Japanese culture and language into their day-to-day lives.

wellness

noun

An active process of making good choices that lead to an overall healthy lifestyle; now co-opted by deranged health obsessives who are happy to promote increasingly outlandish (and scientifically unfounded) methods in order to achieve the Nirvana-like state of *wellness*.

wheelhouse

phrase

Someone's field of knowledge or area of expertise; what you know or understand, or are most capable of doing: *You want a definitive listing of Mandy Moore's top 5 movie roles? That is so totally in my wheelhouse.* Or: *Sorry, Snapchat is just completely outside of my wheelhouse.*

whip

noun

Car, motor vehicle. This is a pretty long bow but, apparently, when cars were first manufactured, the steering wheel was referred to as the 'whip', as a whip was the steering mechanism used on a stagecoach. Running with this historical titbit, and noting that the Mercedes Benz logo looked much like a steering wheel, hip hop artists began referring to their Mercedes as *whips*. The term is now used broadly to refer to any car, regardless of branding.

white knighting

verb

The act of coming to a person's 'rescue', where the act of rescue is unwanted and/or unwarranted; involving yourself in someone else's situation in a thoughtless and intrusive manner.

wicked-

prefix

Very, really, extremely; but be warned, when using wicked you must always put on a terrible Bostonian accent. Examples include *wicked-smart* (really smart), *wicked-cool* (really cool), *wicked-chill* (very relaxed) and *wicked-hot* (super sexy or sexy as hell).

Wiki-hole

noun

The loss of time associated with looking up something on Wikipedia and being inadvertently led into a endless pattern of following links to new, yet increasingly unrelated, information: *I went on Wikipedia to find out how old Zac Efron was, but before I knew it I had read about the history of film-making and then the Russian Revolution and six hours had gone by. I totally fell into a Wiki-hole.*

wind it down

phrase

To calm down or curb your enthusiasm; to lower the tone of something, most especially your state of being, where that tone is heightened in a way that is a little bit too much: *Jace was screaming excitedly at me when he found his first Pokemon, but he was being so loud that I had to ask him to wind it down.*

winning

adjective

Succeeding; popularised by resident madman Charlie Sheen during his very public freakout and split from the hit comedy series *Two and a Half Men*. Whether you have fire-breathing fists, your eyebrows are on fleek or things are just looking up, you're *winning*.

win–win
phrase
A scenario where, no matter what happens, the outcome will be positive. Generally implies you must make a choice between two or more options, and all choices will lead to a positive result. See also **lose–lose**.

woke
adjective
Aware, relevant, ahead of the trends; if you want to stay cool and up (or is it down?) with the zeitgeist, then you need to stay *woke*, which is exactly what this book is for: *Stay woke, peeps.*

word
interjection
Correct, positive affirmation; expression of agreement with the words and sentiment being spoken by a second party: *'That Kendrick Lamar track is bangin.' 'Word.'*

x / xo / xox

noun

Kisses and hugs. Today, signing off with a kiss or a hug has become so ubiquitous that people even include them in work emails: *Thanks for getting that transcript to us in time, Jen. You're a star! xxox*

x factor

noun

An unknown or intangible element that imparts an indescribable quality, generally used to describe a person who is exceptional at something, or someone who is extremely charismatic for reasons you can't define.

Xena

noun

The name of a warrior princess and possibly the greatest television show to ever be made, *Xena* has become a frighteningly popular pet name among owners of rodents across the world. That's right, for whatever reason people are now calling their guinea pigs Xena. Bizarre, we know.

xenophobia

noun

The irrational fear or dislike of people from other countries. While this certainly isn't a modern word, the proliferation of its usage is current, and scary.

xtc

noun

Slang term for the drug ecstasy (MDMA); other common slang terms include *eccies*, *pingers*, *disco biscuits* and *Molly*. If you attempt to use any of these terms your kids will definitely think you're extremely cool.

xvx

noun

Straight edge vegan; straight edge is a hardcore punk subculture where adherents refrain from all forms of recreational drugs, and, in some cases, sex, prescription drugs and caffeine as well. So, one of those but who also doesn't consume animal products.

yarn bombing
verb

A form of street art that
uses knitted or crocheted
yarn to decorate public
spaces (rather than paint,
for instance). A distinctly
hipster phenomenon that
started to gain popularity
in the mid-to-late 2000s.
The practice has since has
lost its underground edge
and has even been co-opted by knitting clubs, with
local governments commissioning works to be displayed
at various locations such as public libraries.

yas / yass
exclamation

Alternative spelling of yes. One morning the internet
woke up and decided to replace the 'e' with an 'a' and
the world hasn't been the same since …

yass queen
interjection

A statement of affirmation and excitement in
celebration of someone or something. Spellings may

vary, with the user adding as many As and Ss as they like depending on their level of excitement – the more the better. *'I just got the job!' 'Yaasssss queen!'*

YMMV
phrase
Initialism of *your mileage may vary*; most commonly used in online forums as an acknowledgement that the opinion of the poster may not be shared by everyone.

YOLO
phrase
Acronym for *you only live once;* the *carpe diem* for the stupidest among us and *the* motto of 2011. Unfortunately, it's still hanging around. Has generally come to be used as an excuse for any misguided action; a verbal shrug: *'Hey, I heard you got hit by a bus while planking on the freeway?' 'Yeah, well, hey … YOLO, man.'*

YouTube
noun
A video-sharing website that hosts content such as music videos, movie trailers, vlogs, video and TV clips, television shows and original video content. Currently the second-most popular website in the world due to the inexplicable popularity of videos of people unboxing new Apple products, reacting to the latest episode of *Game of Thrones*, playing Minecraft or explaining perfect contouring.

yup
adverb
Alternative spelling of *yep*, which is itself an alternative to *yes*. So … *yup*.

-z

suffix

Used to make any word awesome by its simple inclusion; commonly used in place of the letter 's' where it is used to denote a plural, or just whenever: *Hey babez! You have some serious stylez going on. Don't worry about what Tyra said, haterz gonna try and take down your dreamz.*

za

noun

Short for pizza; an idiotic abbreviation popular with males of the jock and/or frat boy variety. Employment of the term is mostly ironic, with the implication being that those who use it are pretty much braindead: *Duuuuuuuude we're meeting at the kegger for some za later.*

zaftig

noun / adjective

A person who is overweight, but carries their weight well. Attractively plump. See also **dad bod**.

zero chill
phrase
To be completely lacking in chill; not relaxed; uptight, nervous, anxious, or in any way uncool: *Donald Trump got zero chill.*

zing
interjection
An exclamation you make after you've said something particularly witty, and you'd really like to point out to everyone just how witty you've been.

zomg
interjection
A variant of OMG, meaning 'oh my god!'; the alternate version to be used in contexts where the intention of OMG is sarcastic or to highlight that someone has stated the obvious: *Ten plus one equals eleven. ZOMG!*

ABBRV

A quick reference guide for commonly used acronyms, initialisms and abbreviations.

2moro	tomorrow
2nte	tonight
AAMOF	as a matter of fact
ADIH	another day in hell
AEAP	as early as possible
AF	as f@#k
AFAIK	as far as I know
AFAIR	as far as I remember / recall
AFK	away from keyboard
AKA	also known as
ALAP	as late as possible
AMA	ask me anything
AND	any day now
ASAP	as soon as possible
ASL	age / sex / location
ATM	at the moment
AYSOS	are you stupid or something?
AYT	are you there?
B3	blah, blah, blah
B4	before
B4YKI	before you know it
BBL	be back later
B/C	because
BD	big deal
BF	boyfriend
BFF	best friends, forever
boyf	boyfriend

BRB	be right back
BRT	be right there
BTAM	be that as it may
BTW	by the way
CSL	can't stop laughing
CTN	can't talk now
CU	see you
CWOT	complete waste of time
CYA	seeya
CYT	see you tomorrow
DAE	does anyone else?
DGA	don't go anywhere
DGAF	don't give a f@#k
DIKU	do I know you?
DKDC	don't know, don't care
DM	direct message
DNC	does not compute
DOC	drug of choice
DQMOT	don't quote me on this
DTF	down to f@#k
ELI5	explain like I'm five
EOD	end of discussion / end of day
EOM	end of message
ETA	edited to add
F2F	face to face
FACK	full acknowledge
FC	fingers crossed
FFS	for f@#k's sake
FKA	formerly known as
FML	f@#k my life
FOAF	friend of a friend
FTFY	fixed that for you
FTW	for the win
FWIW	for what it's worth
FYEO	for your eyes only
FYI	for your information
GF	girlfriend
GIRL	guy in real life
GNOC	get naked on camera

GPOY	gratuitous picture of yourself
GR8	great
GTG	good to go
GTFO	get the f@#k out
GYPO	get your pants off
H8	hate
HAK	hugs and kisses
HIFW	how I felt when
HTH	hope this helps
ICAM	I couldn't agree more
ICYMI	in case you missed it
IDC	I don't care
IDGAF	I don't give a f@#k
IDK	I don't know
IFYP	I feel your pain
IKR	I know, right?
IM	I miss you
IMHO	in my honest / humble opinion
IMO	in my opinion
IOW	in other words
IRL	in real life
ITT	in this thread
IWSN	I want sex now
J/K	just kidding
JSYK	just so you know
JTLYK	just to let you know
KFU	kiss for you
KMN	kill me now
KOTL	kiss on the lips
KPC	keeping parents clueless
kthxbai	okay, thanks, bye
l8r	later
LMAO	laughing my ass off
LMFAO	laughing my f@#king ass off
LMK	let me know
LOL	laughing out loud
MFW	my face when
MIRL	me in real life
MMW	mark my words

MRW	my reaction when
MTFBWU	may the force be with you
MYOB	mind your own business
N/A	not available / applicable
NC	no comment
NIFOC	naked in front of computer
NIMBY	not in my backyard
NM	never mind / nothing much
NNTR	no need to reply
noob / n00b	newbie
NOYB	none of your business
NP	no problem
NSFL	not safe for life
NSFW	not safe for work
NTIM	not that it matters
NVM	never mind
OATUS	on a totally unrelated subject
OIC	oh, I see
OMG	oh my god
OMFG	oh my f@#king god
OMW	on my way
OP	original post / poster
ORLY	oh, really?
OT	off topic
OTL	out to lunch
OTOH	on the other hand
OTP	on the phone
OTT	over the top
PAL	parents are listening
PAW	parents are watching
PEBKAC	problem exists between keyboard and chair
PIR	parent in room
PITA	pain in the ass
PLS	please
PM	private message
PMFI	pardon me for interrupting
POS	parent over shoulder
POV	point of view
PWN	own

QFT	quoted for truth
QT	cutie
RLY	really
RN	right now
ROFL	rolling on the floor laughing
RT	retweet
RU	are you
RUOK	are you okay?
RYS	are you single?
SCNR	sorry, could not resist
SEP	someone else's problem
SFLR	sorry for late reply
SITD	still in the dark
SJW	social justice warrior
SLAP	sounds like a plan
SMH	shaking my head
SO	significant other
SPOC	single point of contact
SRSLY	seriously?
SRY	sorry
STFU	shut the f@#k up
STR8	straight
TBA	to be announced
TBC	to be continued / confirmed
TBH	to be honest
TBT	throwback Thursday
TDTM	talk dirty to me
TGIF	thank God, it's Friday
thx / tnx	thanks
TIA	thanks in advance
TIL	today I learned
TIFU	today I f@#ked up
TL;DR	too long; didn't read
TMA	take my advice
TMI	too much information
TMYL	text me your location
TTG	time to go
TTYL	talk to you later
TWD	texting while driving

TYS	told you so
TYT	take your time
TYVM	thank you very much
UFB	un-f@#king-believable
UOK	you okay?
UR	your / you are
UTM	you tell me
UV	unpleasant visual
W8	wait
WB	welcome back
WFM	works for me
WK	week
W/O	without
WRT	with regard to
WTF	what the f@#k?
WTG	way to go
WTH	what the hell?
WUT	what?
WYCM	will you call me?
WYD	what you doing?
WYWH	wish you were here
YMMD	you made my day
YMMV	your mileage may vary
YOLO	you only live once

Published in 2017 by Smith Street Books
Melbourne | Australia
smithstreetbooks.com

ISBN: 978-1-925418-30-9

The moral rights of the author have been asserted.
CIP data is available from the National Library of Australia

Publisher: Paul McNally
Senior editor: Hannah Koelmeyer, Tusk studio
Design, illustration and layout: Dave Adams

Printed & bound in China by C&C Offset Printing Co., Ltd.

Book 24
10 9 8 7 6 5 4 3 2 1